D0105508

BOUNDLESS

LIGHT

POEMS OF HEALING

BOUNDLESS LIGHT

The Christian Science Publishing Society
210 Massachusetts Avenue, Boston, Massachusetts 02115 USA

Edited by David C. Kennedy and Madora M. Kibbe
Book design by Jerry Rutherford

The Christian Science Publishing Society
210 Massachusetts Avenue, Boston, Massachusetts, 02115 USA
www.christianscience.com
© 2013 The Christian Science Publishing Society

All rights reserved. No part of this book may be reproduced, scanned, or distributed in any printed or electronic form without permission from the publisher (copyright@csps.com).

Works cited and referenced—written by Mary Baker Eddy and published by the Christian Science Board of Directors:
Manual of The Mother Church (abbreviated *Manual*)
Miscellaneous Writings: 1883–1896 (abbreviated *Miscellaneous Writings*)
Science and Health with Key to the Scriptures (abbreviated *Science and Health*)

ISBN 978-0-87510-495-9
G750B51550EN

Printed in the United States of America
First Edition · Second Printing

CONTENTS

PRAYER

THE HEALING POWER OF DIVINE LOVE

THE TOUCH DIVINE

POISED on wings of filigree,
    Patterned with deft artistry,
Poems are such fragile things
    In their flight.
Yet, with all their gentle ways,
They exert a power that sways,
Oftentimes, the fate of kings
    By their might.

But the loveliest of all
Is a poem I recall
Bearing solace as it sings
    In the night.
Through its healing touch divine,
In accord with Love's design,
Comes the Christ, whose message brings
    Boundless light.

—Jean Hazel Allen

INTRODUCTION

"Let there be light"

Whether expressed in prose or in verse, spiritual light heals. The source of this light is God—the divine Principle of being, the Father-Mother of all, the infinite Truth forever revealing itself. The Psalmist sang of God, "...with thee is the fountain of life: in thy light shall we see light." (Psalm 36:9)

No one book could possibly collect all of the poetry that has encouraged and healed people over the past hundred years. Contained in this volume, *Boundless Light*, is a sampling of poems published in the *Christian Science Sentinel* and *The Christian Science Journal* over a number of decades. The voices of these poems are varied. But they speak a common message: the healing power of God and its application in Christian Science.

However inspired or beautifully written, these poems are not an end in themselves. As was their original purpose when first published, they are intended to be a light on the path of the reader leading to a clearer comprehension of Spirit and man's oneness with God, who is infinite Spirit. Their intent is not to merely talk about healing but to help bring healing. "The words of divine Science find their immortality in deeds," writes Mary Baker Eddy, the Discoverer and Founder of Christian Science, "for their Principle heals the sick and spiritualizes humanity." (*Science and Health* 354:9)

We hope these poems will encourage, inspire, and comfort those who read them.

A PRAYER FOR POETS

*T*HIS is highest poetry:
    to help the crippled walk,
to aid the deaf to hear,
to free the dumb to talk.

These are the greatest poems:
a blind one made to see,
mourning turned to laughter,
a lame child healed and free.

May we walk on, O Master,
where your own feet have trod,
to learn eternal rhythms—
the poetry of God.

—Arthur L. Hendriks

God's Supremacy

PURE MIND

GOD is pure Mind; He does not work through matter.
Mind needs no outside medium to express
its nature. All that Mind creates is wholly
of mental and spiritual substance, nothing less.

Man is pure Mind's idea. Not made from matter,
man needs no physical basis to sustain
his individual life. Mind's man and woman
pure thought in Mind eternally remain.

The pure ideas of Mind are not polluted,
infected, poisoned, pressured, fractured, strained
by matter. Their only atmosphere is boundless
intelligence, self-renewed and self-contained.

Pure Mind, controlling all in ordered action,
governs alike the atom and the star.
Wherever thought consents and hearts are willing,
its instant healings and adjustings are.

Mind has no place for matter in its eternal
purpose. But wholly spiritual, wholly good,
pure Mind's ideas, coperfect with their Maker,
unfold within pure Mind's infinitude.

— Peter J. Henniker-Heaton

VISION

"LORD, ... open his eyes, that he may see,"*
    The mighty prophet prayed.
Send not armies great and strong,
Neither strength to battle wrong,
But lift his vision to behold
Thy truth already here,
The legions of omnipotence,
The hosts of Thy deliverance.

Awake, O man, and know
Love's all-embracing sphere.

Lord, open my eyes that I may see
Thy presence everywhere,
My dwelling circled by Thy might,
My mountaintop aflame with light,
The shining sentinels of Thy love
Triumphant in this hour.
For Thou with me art greater far
Than all the seeming evils are.

Be still, O heart, and trust
His omnipresent power.

—Elizabeth Glass Barlow

* See II Kings 6:15–17

GOD'S DAY

"THIS is the day which the Lord hath made;
    we will rejoice
and be glad in it,"* the Psalmist said.
    Heed now his voice.

This is the day when Mind beholds
    its perfect plan—
divine intelligence unfolds
    in idea, man.

The day when Spirit's cleansing ray
    of truth dispels
belief in matter's brash display;
    shows all is well.

The day when Soul supreme reflects
    all beauty, grace;
reveals man's selfhood pure; rejects
    the senses' farce.

This is the day of Principle's
    wise government
controlling all—invincible,
    omnipotent.

The day when Life divine shows forth
    itself in life
untouched by illness, age, or death
    and free from strife.

The day when Truth alone maintains
    the rule of right,
annulling error's darkest claims
    with piercing light.

This is the day that Love inspires
    with liberty;
all fear dissolves, all hate expires,
    and we are free.

— David C. Driver

*Psalm 118:24

ASSURANCE

YOU can trust God to be good.
You yourself would
Help a friend,
And you yourself send
Good to those you love.
Can you expect of
God anything less
Than tenderness?
The smallest ray supplies,
To open eyes,
Proof of day begun—
Assurance of the sun.

— Pearl Strachan Hurd

THE PANOPLY

*G*OD'S is the hand that moves and weaves
the thoughts we wear in this bright hour:
their threads are woven into one
robe of prayer …
To trace
the loveliness of Principle, which falls
about our days as laws of light, is to love
the panoply of His renewing grace.

— *Godfrey John*

TRUSTING

*M*UST we lend a hand
      to guide the orbiting moon?
Must we orchestrate the stars at night?
The Mind that holds the sparrow and all worlds
      Will every moment care for you aright.

— David C. Kennedy

SUDDEN LIGHT
IN DARKNESS

ISTEN—
marvel!

No collision shattering
status quo; instead
the peace that knows
that nothing's nothing,

for All
is all!

— *Richard Henry Lee*

O Thou
UNCHANGING Truth

O THOU unchanging Truth, whose facts eternal
give us the courage to outface the storm,
to rise against the senses' swift alarm
and stand unmoved at Spirit's high tribunal,
Thy Word acquits us and Thy Word is final.

O Thou abundant Life, whose freshness daily
admits no common round, no dull routine,
this is our joy and this our discipline,
to take Thy gift of life and use it fully;
this is our highest task, to spend it freely.

O boundless Love, forever undiminished,
how far and little seems the lie of pain.
We were with Thee, before the world began,
and shall be with Thee, when the world has vanished;
Thy work is perfect and Thy work is finished.

— Peter J. Henniker-Heaton

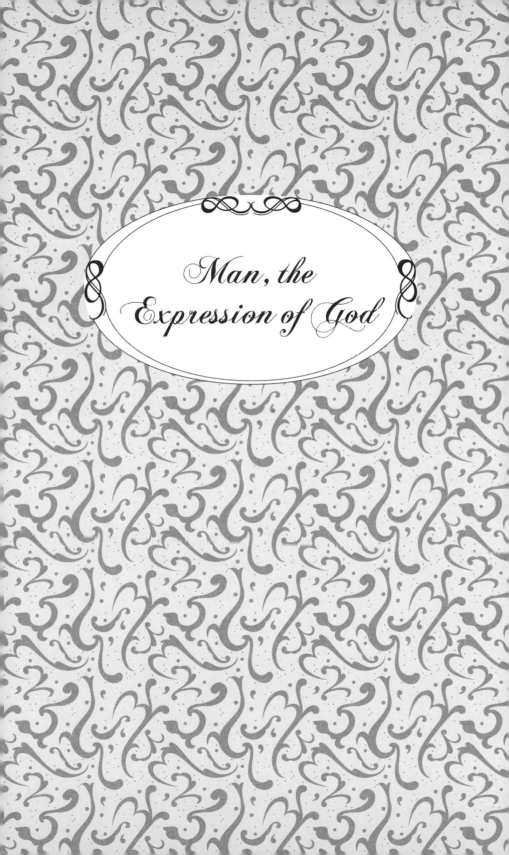

Man, the Expression of God

THE AUTHOR OF OUR LIVES

*I*T was a cheerless script,
 that mortal tale—
 claiming to be *my* past, *my* story.

A litany of missed chances, condemnation, and regret.
With paragraphs of pain too graphic to forget.

I didn't know there were different pages, an altogether
 different book.

Until I was compelled to look—

And saw my name written on a cover, pure white,
And felt my heart leap up—

... could it be true?

The chapter titles were startling, new—
Yet something deep inside ... *remembered:*

"You are my beloved daughter, in whom
 I am well pleased."
"Rejoice and be exceedingly glad."
"You are the light of the world."

On each page, irrefutable proof—
 of my beautiful selfhood,
 untainted substance,
 resounding innocence,
 eternal worth.

Past and future, dissolved into *now*,
One seamless account, fresh and alive.

A volume of love, bearing Love's pure inscription,

The *real* story ... by the Author of our lives.

—Melanie L. Daglian

(Quotations paraphrase Luke 3:22, Matthew 5:12, 14)

THE DIAMOND

A DIAMOND in a darkened room
Is nothing but a stone.
It needs the light to sparkle—
It cannot shine alone.

So raise the shades of darkened sense,
And let Christ's light shine through.
God's perfect gem is always there—
Immortal, sin-free you.

— William J. Byrne

PERFECT REFLECTION

*L*OOKING deep into the
reflection in the lake
and taking a head count,
nothing was missing.

Every cloud, tree, leaf, blade of grass,
every sailboat, duck, bird,
nothing was missing,
the reflection mirrored it all.

A reflection can't
delete some objects
and add others;
reflection is exact.

Looking deep into God,
man is His reflected image.
Nothing is missing,
the reflection mirrors All.

— *Melissa Raber*

A MAN TOOK UP HIS BED

WHOEVER lies at Bethesda
(the hours drifting away)
looking for visions and miracles
can begin to arise this day.

Though the waters may seem to be troubled
by an angel out of the sky
the crowds cannot hold you back at all
from your healing, as they surge by.

There is nothing to keep you from the Christ
as you search your heart anew.
Your prayer and longing will bring you
to a knowledge of what is true:

You are the flawless child of God,
who loves you and keeps you sound;
you have always walked in Love and Life
and on holy ground.

So lift up your thought to this healing truth
as a man once took up his bed.
Will you lie at the pool of Bethesda
or rise up and walk instead?

—John Cuno

THY BIRTHRIGHT

FORGET not who thou art, thou son of God,
  For God demands reflection pure of thee;
Thy heritage is goodly, and thy home
  Is in the covert of infinity.

Thou art the child of Spirit, sinless, pure;
  Thine is a perfect beauty, born of Soul;
Wholeness is thine, and health, and energy.
  For is not God, thy Father, perfect, whole?

Thine understanding, too, doth come from God.
  For in that Mind, magnificent and clear,
Wast thou conceived of Him, a pure idea,
  Unhampered by the flesh, or doubt, or fear.

So now look up into God's holy light
  And greet with fearless joy each coming day.
Of royal birth, a King's own child, art thou—
  And God is thine, and thou art God's alway.

— *Mildred Spring Case*

TRUE RECORD

*F*ORMS cannot touch man. He is out of reach
of what material documents may declare.
Certificates of birth cannot attach
age to immortal being. Man's life was here
before the shadow of the flesh appeared,
and when the shadow of the flesh is gone,
still will shine forth, radiant and unimpaired.
Records of death refer not to God's son.

In such and such a place and of such parents,
graded particulars both good and bad,
some register may assert. This false appearance,
mortality's ancient birth-wrong, never had
reference to man, child of the Father-Mother
Spirit. Man's citizenship forever is
in the boundless realm of heaven; he knows no other
inheritance but good, all that God has.

No record of education, worse or better,
experience, training, past employment, can
limit man's opportunities or fetter
God's ever-unfolding purpose for His son.
No medical sheet can mask our inviolate wholeness,
no criminal record blemish our innocence.
The Christ, the resistless Word, affirms good's allness,
correcting flimsy records of physical sense.

"Let us make man," God said. And God created
man in His image, perfect, flawless, whole.
This is the changeless record that antedated
all records of the flesh and mortal ill.
This is the record that, steadfastly accepted,
has power to heal, to free, to override
all human forms, and stands uninterrupted—
man's perfect record, divinely certified.

—Peter J. Henniker-Heaton

THE PRESENT DAY
OF MIRACLES

*I*N full accordance with God's law
the miracle fulfills His plan.
This will explain the thing I saw:
that hand stretched forth without a flaw.
Such healings prove God's will for man.

It's natural for man to be
all His creator would design.
Perfection must be His decree
for His own image. How could He
create His child less than divine?

Let us accept His work as done!
Let us our Father's law enforce!
Let us know law and Love are one,
holding us safely, as the sun
is held, established in its course.

Then daily miracles will prove
the law of God the only power.
Then all will be secure in Love,
rejoicing in the coming of
the Christ to earth. God speed the hour!

                    —*Jane M. Crisp*

His shining light

For many years I wiped and scrubbed
and rubbed the windowpane I thought was me
to be a clear transparency
for Truth.
But I was never crystal-clear
nor felt my victory quite so near
as when I learned that man is not
transparency.
He's light!
Much more than spots where God shines through,
we are His shining, bright and true.

— *David Littlefield Horn*

WRITTEN IN HEAVEN!*

*Y*OU are
not what appearance says you are:
a victim labeled
accident or
circumstance
encrypted in some bio-code
of earthly dust or clay.

You are
the named
intended
heir
of
God,
inscribed above.
Omnipotence
records
your name
with flourishes
of
love!

— *Bettie Gray House*

THE WEDDING

I DO.
I'm willing
To be wedded
To my perfect selfhood.

Divorced from dualism's subtle sway,
Through with fruitless wanderings,
I do—as of this day—
Take for my very life
The spiritual perfection
That has ever been mine
As God's own dear reflection.

—*Doris Lubin*

THE SINGLE EYE

IF thine eye be single*
    (Thy body full of light),
Good and bad can't mingle;
Day can't turn to night.

Thy body full of light
(All reflected glory)!
Day can't turn to night;
Time can't end the story.

All reflected glory!
(Selfhood perfect, pure.)
Time can't end the story;
Vision must endure.

Selfhood perfect, pure
(Good and bad can't mingle).
Vision must endure—
If thine eye be single.

—*Doris Kerns Quinn*

*See Matthew 6:22

BE STILL, MY HEART

BE still, my heart: you rest in Love divine;
      God's gracious touch has silenced grief and pain.
His timeless Christ has ordered no decline;
In changeless being shall your health remain.
Be still, my heart: your faithful only Friend
Secures your joyful voyage without end.

Be still, my heart: of present glories sing
Instead of mourning for a troubled past.
Replace sad tunes with melodies that ring
Of God's rich mercy and of blessings vast.
Be still, my heart: the winds and waves recede
When to His angel voices you give heed.

Be still, my heart: our Father casts out fears,
Assuring you of God and man at one;
And in that oneness here and now appears
His everlasting life, with death outdone.
Be still, my heart: no lies, no tears, no curse
Can mar the rhythm of His universe.

— Harold Rogers

NOBLE ENDEAVOR

Be a sculptor
          every day
Mold and chisel thought
          following your model,
                    Christ.

Carve away
     unneeded, unbelonging
                    mortal sense

See the form
          God's image
                    appearing in you

In him
     in her
               in every one.

— *Geraldine Schiering*

Thought Opens to Healing

HEALING

*W*HEN thought grew calm and human
will was silent,
the healing came,
gentle and natural as an opening flower.
Within the freedom of true self-
surrender,
we feel the healing touch of Love's
all-power.

— Greta Claxton

RESTORATION

*I*S inspiration lost? Find gratitude,
  And let her lead you gently by the hand.
Filling the vacuum of your solitude,
She will guide you straightly to her friend.
For gratitude and inspiration dwell together,
Their home the humble heart that, trusting, waits,
Patient and strong in bright or stormy weather,
Where love its banner lifts above its gates.

If you have lost expectancy of healing,
Be grateful for perfection's changelessness.
Regarding not material sense's feeling,
Your vision lift in glad perceptiveness.
The shock of pain with holy courage meet;
None are defeated who own not defeat.

If health should seem the focus of ambition,
Then seek a dearer, more enduring goal;
Let love for God and man your thought condition,
And yearning find completion safe in Soul.
Let waiting times be times of dedication
To seek afresh the purposes of Love,
And then both health and also inspiration
Truth's allness and your steadfastness will prove.

Choose well your path, and do not vacillate
Between the things of matter and of Spirit.
Know what is real, and lo, emancipate,
You walk with God, and all His good inherit.
But whether hope burns high, or is subdued,
Companion still with faithful gratitude.

— *Rosemary C. Cobham*

I'D RATHER GIVE
AUDIENCE TO SPIRIT

I REALLY wasn't enjoying the show
playing on my stage of consciousness—
sad, depressing, even frightening,
and with a cast of characters
no one could love.

"The show must go on." It must?
Must something so bad have a good run?
Then I had an angel of an idea:
I stopped watching; took away the audience.
And the show closed!

— Elizabeth Bice Luerssen

Three l's for life

*L*EAN on the sustaining infinite
And blessings will be yours.*
Lean not on person, place, or thing
Or economic laws;
But lean upon all-blessing God
Who will all needs supply
And give to all abundant good
That money cannot buy.

Let the reign of Truth and Life,*
The reign of Love divine,
Be now established within me
To show God's clear design
Of Oneness, indivisible,
Of He and me as one,
As water is to ocean,
As sunbeam is to sun.

Love with a heart of tenderness
Your enemies and friends;
However hard this may appear
It's the quality that mends.
For Love is God in action,
A presence that is felt;
A healing and a saving power
That will all discord melt.

So **lean**, and **let**, and **love**,
This is the balanced Way;
It's free from self-will, pressure, stress,
It welcomes in God's day;
The leaning is so gentle,
The letting is so free,
And loving is the only way
To think, and speak, and **be**.

—Jill Gooding

* See *Science and Health,* p. vii; *Manual,* p. 41

ASK SOON

THERE'S one question
you've got to ask
yourself soon.
It's this:

"Do I want to find and feel
the fresh truth
of Christian Science
over again—to be absorbed
with this light—*more* than I want
to lose the dark
of pain or of grief, of crisis or hate?"

Ask soon.

I've seen
lives made fully free
out of the right
answer to that one.

— *Godfrey John*

Your testimony

*W*HAT you said last night
moved like a clean fresh wind
to scatter clouds, bring gentle rain
to parched hope.
And afterward, a clear shining,
bright and pure,
revealing God's present goodness
never lost to me.

This morning, the wind still softly stirs
—fresh as flower—

Thank you, friend, for sharing, caring,
   healing me!

  — *Cora Slaughter*

HOME

"IN self we trust," my motto was;
My coin, philosophy.
My citadel, pure reason's shell,
My pearl, the knowledge tree.

Cool intellect and I inspected
Atoms, history, art:
(At ego's call, the walls would fall,
The whole reveal the part).

Then suddenly, extremity
Turned pride's poor stone to sand;
As knowledge slipped my frightened grip,
I reached with humbled hand

And felt the touch that breaks the crutch
Of matter: "All is Mind,"*
One Truth revealed, all error healed,
Seek here, and ye shall find!

With one short step from self I leapt
And found I could not fall,
For in that space the swift embrace
Of Love held me—and all!

—*Ann C. Stewart*

*Miscellaneous Writings, p. 286

Qualities
That Heal

DON'T GIVE UP!

*L*ET love go ahead of
your army of faith
and circle those adamant walls
(the limits that call themselves you).
Keep moving. Keep marching.
For seven rounds of persistence.
Blast the trumpet.
Claim your dominion.
Wear that God-bestowed crown.

Then watch those walls
Come tumbling down!

— Elizabeth Glass Barlow

THE GARMENT OF GRATITUDE

NEVER leave it in the closet—
    that is not its proper place—
let it clothe your total being.
    Wear it with unfettered grace—

formed of fabric soft as zephyr
    yet as strong as welded steel,
woven with the warp of promise
    crossed with woof of heaven's seal.

Wear it always, every moment
    knowing nothing can destroy
its seamless, flawless, sure protection.
    Wear it with unmeasured joy!

—Virginia L. Scott

REWARD

ONLY the pure are happy;
Only the just have peace.
God's laws require obedience
Before they bring release.

— Wilhelmina Belle Barnes

THE LETTING IS ALL

IT'S all about the letting
not the getting, grabbing
pushing, pulling
trying to do more, or go, go where?
You're there, already there, in His arms.

It's all about the letting and
the giving and forgiving
and the living in the light of Love.
Don't shove, don't hold your breath,
you're being held right now.
How? By love, again and always, Love.

It's all about the letting, yes,
that's the hardest part, I guess,
not outlining, designing, or even inclining
but communing with God
listening, active listening.
It's really difficult sometimes, and
takes a lot of effort
but, when you get it, it's really effort-less.
Pray more, say less.
Wait, stand, watch, breathe.

Like sunrise, like rainbow, it will happen,
your answer will find you
if you let it
if you let.

— *Madora M. Kibbe*

COMFORTED

THERE was no way, it seemed, to lift the stone
      That was my heart; no way, it seemed, to write
The beauty I so loved. *Alone, alone,*
   Dinned in my ears; and morning, noon, and night
Weighted the hours, darkened dawn, and stole
   All color from the world. (My lawless thought
Meant spiritual anarchy, for to be whole
   I knew well where to turn, yet I would not.)

At last I bowed my stubborn head and wept,
   "Father, forgive me for ignoring You.
Your guidance, love, and strength have always kept
   Me joyous … free … atop a high plateau."

Then comforted, recalling lessons learned,
I knew His truth again would be confirmed.

                 — *Margery Todahl Blokhine*

ON GENTLE WORD

OH, let it never bear a sting—
the thought you think. Make it a bird!
Oh, feather it with love, and wing
it carefully on gentle word.
Then it will rise and sweetly sing,
and bless wherever it is heard.

—*Althea Brooks Hollenbeck*

VICTORY

NOT only in the peaceful countryside
 Do blackbirds sing.
In city's trafficking
You'll hear them
Through the traffic's din.
They will, I'm told,
Sing even on a battlefield.

Brave and grateful hearts
Make no conditions.
You will hear their song
Pealing spontaneously long
Before healing is apparent.
Their joy inherent,
They wait not on the dawn,
They sing it on.
This they know—
God made man perfect, and maintains him so.
And so they sing.

To songs of gratitude illusions yield;
Gone is the battlefield.

      — Rosemary C. Cobham

My daily watch

I AM the keeper of the temple gate
    of consciousness;
    no thought can pass
except with my consent.

Love and I will halt each messenger
    to consciousness,
    and bar the door,
except to the heaven-sent.

— Carol Earle Chapin

PATIENCE

PATIENCE isn't
Mourning in the dark,
Waiting for light.
It is joy in every moment:
Constant consciousness of right.

—Lynne Cook

CLIMBING

WHEN I began the climb
From sense to Soul
My step was buoyant, and
With new-found truth
I swept the path
Of all that hindered
          the upward journey.

With heat of noontime
The brambles thickened
And seldom yielded
Without a struggle;
Stumbling and rising,
Slowly I plodded
          on toward the summit.

Then the pathway faded,
And waist-deep I stood
In underbrush; the forest
Turned the day to night.
Disheartened and afraid,
Blind with self-pity,
          like Hagar, weeping,

I heard God's voice and rose,
Followed His guiding,
And I emerged at last
Far up the mountain;
And to my glad surprise
Found that, through fear and doubt,
          I had been climbing.

— Ruby M. Drogseth

LISTENING

*A*RE you listening, really listening?
    Or do your words like droplets in a waterfall
  spill over in their eagerness
  to reach the Father's ear—
  so that you cannot hear
      His voice,
that still, small voice
    that transcends human fear?

If you are listening, really listening
    in calm and quiet expectancy,
your Father's loving message will reach receptive thought,
    and either suddenly or gradually
    through mortal mind's cacophony
you'll hear the truth you sought.

— Peggy Jean Goodrum

THE ANSWER

IN the words of the young man whom Jesus met,
  She too asked: "Lord, 'what lack I yet?'
What do I need to heal this case
And error's picture to erase?
Do I need more humility,
More meekness, and less vanity?
Lack I still yet a motive pure,
A little faith that will endure?
Is it more gratitude I need,
More honesty of thought and deed?
What is my need, all else above?"
The answer came, "To love, to love!"

— Maxine Le Pelley

Prayer

THOROUGHNESS

*L*ET me be thorough in my work
Like Joshua and his people—
Not slipshod, halfway
But seven times around the wall
Till I see the evil fall.

Let me be thorough also in forgiveness—
Not halfhearted
Holding something back.
Not merely seven times.
I must do better

For the Master said
"Seventy times seven."
Let my love be of the heart
Not just the head
Then I'll find the kingdom of God's heaven.

—*Doris Kerns Quinn*

SUCH A DIFFERENCE

SUCH a difference
   between deceiver and Redeemer—
the one who says I,
and the one who says,
"As I hear, I speak."

Such a difference
between asking,
"Do I really know
all that I'm declaring?" and
receiving all God is
asking me to think.

Such a difference
between my will and ...
"Thy kingdom come."

—*Allison W. Phinney*

DESIRE

*M*Y one desire, dear Lord, with Thee to walk;
  And in that sweet communion, day by day,
So quickened be, that I may hear Thee talk,
  And garner closely all that Thou would'st say.

While in that sweet converse, as friend to friend,
  What boundless love would'st Thou to me unfold,
And truths reveal, whose worth should far transcend
  Earth's rarest gems or priceless gifts of gold.

Within that hallowed atmosphere with Thee,
  My every thought with purest love imbued,
I would rejoice—nor power in evil see—
  And let my deeds attest my gratitude.

—E. Jewel Robinson

Integrity's Quiet Question

IF it feels difficult to pray
    (awareness of God seems far away)
and rehearsals of "truth-words"
    don't convey
        much of anything,
try integrity's quiet question:
    "What do I really desire?"

Then, hush!
    Brush off whining "…but I can't hear His voice."
    Build a silent haven for your choice
        to glorify good.
    Relying on Love's tender might,
        hold to Truth's clear light.

Adore good alone!
    And as you find your one desire is
        to do Love's will,
        stay still.

Now allow in your day the space to obey.

— *Beverly Jean Scott*

INSPIRED DEFIANCE

*S*HARP pain turned thought
  to God.
I sought
release from fear
by realization clear
of God's All-power.

Deep prayer for light
brought promise bright;
thought soared serene
above the dream
of matter's lies
and "reason whys."

Then came the call
"Don't just deny…
defy!"
for God is All.

So I complied,
pain, lies, defied—
not just denied.

Then Truth obeyed
was acted on,
and lo
all pain was gone …
stayed gone!

God proved supreme,
matter seen *just dream.*
Health found intact,
spiritual fact.

—*Hugh K. Fraser*

JUST WHAT IS HEALING?

HEALING is not a clever alteration
        or uninspired, lazy toying
with our mortal dreams.

Real healing is quickened revealing
of man's intact purity—
inspiration *felt*,
melting callous mortal laws.

Healing reveals in fresh, sharp focus—
deep, timeless, and exact—
spiritual fact!

                                        —*Brett L. Stafford*

Realm of Prayer

SEEK not a better mortal care,
however needed it may seem;
but have a higher goal for prayer—
resolve to break the dream.

When healing's grace is what is sought,
seek first of all immortal thought.

— Lyle M. Crist

COUNSEL

IN your dark night
　　Do not go down into the valley.
It would be easy, but then
There would only be
The long climb out again.

It would be wise
To stay up on the height;
The stars are bright,
And from there one can see
An earlier sunrise.

—Alan W. Thwaites

HOMECOMING

"Lord, thou hast been our dwelling place in all generations." [1]

CHRIST'S healing influence
Comes to lift my heart
Above material sense and sadness.

It leads me to holy mount of God
Where I bow before Soul;
I listen.

"Be still, and know that I am God." [2]
"Be silent, O all flesh, before the Lord." [3]

Be silent, lie of life in matter.
Be still.

Heavenly winds blow.
Suffering sense departs,
Surrenders to Christly calm.

Angel truths descend
To cleanse my thought of cherished hurt
And bathe it in God's grace.

In morning light of Love
I look with child-eyes
To see all things made new
(A mortal past was never true).

No ties of flesh
Bind God's beloved
To sickness, sin, or pain.

His sons and daughters,
All safe and pure,
Forever live in Spirit—
Dwelling of changeless love and joy,
Home of perfect peace.

— Marjorie Russell Tis

[1] Psalm 90:1
[2] Psalm 46:10
[3] Zechariah 2:13

THE PRIZE

*L*IKE the dove that Noah sent forth
from his ark,
Christly prayer
right here and now
is sure to return
with olive-leafed prize.
No guessing.
Secure in Mind's flawless accuracy,
Law-fulfilling prayer foreseals
the triumph:
Christian Science heals!

— *Maxine Le Pelley*

The Healing
Power of
Divine Love

LOVE'S EVER-PRESENCE

THERE is a presence walks with us
    On every pathless way,
A light outshining midday sun
    However dark the day.

We reach our hand—and feel God near;
    We cry—and He replies;
We open eyes that sense had dimmed,
    We stretch our wings and rise

Above the mist, above the dark,
    Above the threats of fear,
Upheld by Love that never fails
    And is forever near.

We cannot stray beyond Love's care,
    For Love does fill all space;
And where we go the path is marked
    By angels of Love's grace.

—Kathryn Paulson Grounds

GOD'S MOTHER LOVE

GOD'S mother love broods over all! Have I
necessities His love will not supply
who measures not one need as great or small,
but even tends the sparrow at its fall?
God's mother love my strength will ever be
which tends us both alike—the bird and me!

—Althea Brooks Hollenbeck

LOVE NEVER FAILS

*D*ID Jesus ask the palsied man if he were fit for
    prayer,
When at the pool of Bethesda he saw him lying there?
Did he ignore the man's desire for health and happiness,
Or think mayhap some stubbornness made him unfit to
    bless?

No! Jesus, Christly king of love, beheld the perfect one;
The light of Truth shone clear to him upon his Father's
    son.
Not all the error in the world, nor sin in Satan's hell,
Could stem the flowing tide of love that made that sick
    man well.

— *Wilfred Kermode*

EVER HIGHER

STIFF winds give a strong lift,
    as the unseen hand of Love
        carries the eagle into the purest spheres.

Do unrelenting winds of grief pour in
    where yearning hope clings to a light still dim?
        Then look upward—
        for even now Love lifts us into sweeter joys
        that never will be lost.

Do commanding tasks sweep down on us
    more strongly than our strength can grasp?
        Then look upward—
        for even now Love lifts us into newborn powers
        all fresh, unfailing, found in Soul.

Do daily calls for unselfed toil
    exhaust a well gone dry?
        Then devotion must move higher—
        and Love will fill our cup with patience, bliss,
           and newfound freedom welling up within.

Has blustery fear pushed in on us
    to make us doubt our cherished stance?
        Then dear one, *still look upward*—
        for even now Love's arms are all around and
        underneath,
           we can't fall through.

Taking wings of courage we are lifted—each and every
one—
    above ourselves, to find beyond the grimmest clouds
    the radiant face of Love.

—David C. Kennedy

Regeneration und Restoration

More than a quilt

THE light of Christ is not a patchwork quilt
It is a seamless garment
So we cannot be satisfied
with stitching our lives together
into pleasant little patterns
The only real pattern
is the one of transfiguration
The light of Christ is a transformer
not a seamstress
The Christ not only mends, it restores
and renews and reveals what already always has been
And every time we part with
our preconceived pieces,
our this-is-how-it-should-work-out outlook
we are blessed
and robed in light,
a light that also warms the world,
the Christ light, which is not a quilt but
the Comforter.

— *Madora M. Kibbe*

ANANIAS*

" *I* HEARD you, Lord: '*Heal him.*'
But ... may I say a word?
This Saul—haven't I heard
about Jerusalem
and how he scorched us there—
the violence, terror, despair?"

Ananias,
what matters to us
nineteen centuries since
is that you shattered such logic
and listened.
Routing your own resistance, you trusted,
freeing the verse of your heart
with the rhythm of intuition.
Love-led, you dared face hatred with compassion.

Not that you didn't question—
we all have. But out of that blaze
you came, wide-eyed and childlike,
to uncritical innocence.

Without your kind, the Sauls would be
nothing
but blind.

— *Rushworth M. Kidder*

*See Acts 9:10–18

BE COLUMBUS!

*Y*OU, homeless, lost, face to face
   with lust, disgust, despair, in the city streets;
you, young girl, hoping, believing
in what is truest and timeless about you—
purity, dignity, love—
you, innocent!

You, son, on the run, your gun discarded,
in refuge finding a dying potted plant
and nourishing it as dusk closes in,
then smiling at its tiny leaves as they lift
at last to meet you in the morning shadows—
you, innocent!

Innocence has no age.
Innocence cannot die.
For each of us
God pours His fresh quenchless love.
Look up. It's not too late.
In each of us
lies the promised land—the consciousness
where innocence flowers in immunity.

Oh son, daughter, comrade—live
calmly, courageously. What is happening?
Christ is happening:
see, in you now looms a new
land of undiscovered destiny.

You, innocent—be Columbus
to this stainless continent of light!

— *Godfrey John*

"DESIRE IS PRAYER"[*]

ERE dawn her saffron sails unfurled,
    Or timid night-wraiths fled away,
The penitent looked up and cried:
My Father, I would learn to pray.

For I have followed winding paths,
My feet besmirched with miry clay,
Sin-tired and penitent I come—
Grant, Lord, that I may learn to pray.

Give me not words but thoughts so pure
That they as buoyant wings may bear
My song of praise aloft to Thee,
And Thy omniscience declare.

Teach me to frame my prayer with deeds,
With tender words, with helping hand,
Before disdain continue kind,
Nor doubt that Thou wilt understand.

Create in me a thirst for good,
A yearning for those gifts divine
Thou hast for me, gifts mine to take.
Reflecting Thee, I prove them mine.

So vigilant is Love divine,
God's voice was heard ere golden day:
Housed in thine heart are pure desires,
Already thou hast learned to pray.

— E. Jewel Robinson

Science and Health, p. 1

TRANSFORMATION

IN letting in the light of Truth,
    Where darkness long has been,
We may disclose a startling sin
    And wish 'twere dark again.

But dwelling in this new-found light,
    The self we had concealed
Is found, as sense of sin is lost
    And Life and Truth revealed.

We need not sorrow for the sins
    That Truth has brought to view,
But grateful be that this same Truth
    Unfolds a self that's new.

— Flora A. Bixby

Trials, Proofs of God's Care

THE CHRIST APPEARS

*T*HE fourth watch—
    Can seem the darkest hour of the night,
When sea is tempest-tossed

The fourth watch—
When Jesus came
Walking on the sea

Our fourth watch—
That dark moment
When all seems turbulent
Is when the Christ appears.

— Eleanor Henderson Buser

"It never was"

"It cannot be," "It never was,"
Yet error lingered on,
'Til Love divine dissolved the lie
And "never was" was gone.

No shots were fired, no swords unsheathed,
No battle lines were drawn,
As perfect Life was realized.
This brought a perfect dawn.

What seemed like time was *progress*,
What seemed like meekness, *might*.
The joy of demonstration came—
I felt the dove alight!

— *Doris June Jack*

VICTORY

So subtly tempted, Lord, was I
To hearken to the serpent's lie;
But like a still small voice I heard
Throughout that fiery trial Thy Word,
Which came as pure, uplifted thought,
Dissolving that which was not wrought
By Thee, and therefore could not be
A law or power beguiling me.

—Doris A. Lewis

JOY FREES

IN our tribulation
    we must remember to rejoice.
Paul did it. He even
lifted up his voice and sang
in prison,
in the midnight hour.

Can we do less?
Let us confess
(in our prisons of poverty,
sorrow, loss, temptation)
we too can break the bonds—
however strong.
We too can break the bonds
with rejoicing
in our midnight song.

No prison walls can stand
before a joyful heart
making its melody
in praise of God.

Joy crumbles the walls,
breaks the chains,

sets us free.

—Doris Kerns Quinn

AWAKE!

THE world says that I walk alone—
    How little does it know!
The world keeps sounding in my ears
Its own uncertain doubts and fears,
Its dread of what the passing years
    May hold, as on I go.

The world says that I walk alone—
    How little can it tell!
Life points the shining, upward way,
Truth guides and guards my path today,
Love gently whispers, Come what may,
    He doeth all things well.

The world says that I walk alone—
    How little does it see!
Each hour new assurance brings,
My heart looks up, and softly sings,
I feel the touch of angel wings
    Forever close to me.

God's children never are alone,
    No matter how it seems.
A Love beyond all human ken,
Beyond all words of tongue or pen,
Is here to heal each heartache—when
    We waken from our dreams!

                    — *Louise Knight Wheatley Cook*

I CAN TELL YOU THIS…

I CAN tell you this…
not my wisdom—
others have told it—
Daniel, the Psalmist,
Jacob, Stephen.

When the darkness comes down
like an Arctic night, the
daylight's squeezed out,
supposedly nothing to know,
some angel comes, says,
"O man greatly beloved,"*
pulls you up from your knees.

You don't even have to see
a dawn, a change of times or
season, the real
sings again in you—in spite of
reasons—just God's
light not gone, but there,
and more than ever
everywhere.

—Allison W. Phinney

*See Daniel 10:10, 11

Praying
for Others

"THE TRUTH SHALL MAKE YOU FREE"*

(Letter to a Christian Science practitioner)

*M*OVED *with compassion ...*
you met me where I am
(not where I thought I was).

You took me by the hand
and never let me go.
Beheld me as the
apple of His eye ...*

You saw the me
I couldn't seem to see myself
and held me in the secret place
I'd really never left.

You knew me face to face
with God,
embraced in Love,
untouched by time,
until there was not one speck left for me to see
save Soul's radiance mirrored back at me.

Amazed in grace.
Unblemished.
Spotless.
Free!

— *Bonnie MacDonald*

*See John 8:32; Mark 1:41; Deuteronomy 32:10

THE VOICE OF TRUTH

OT in the earthquake or the flame,
   The wracking wind, or violence, came
   The voice of Truth—omnipotence.
But in the stillness and the calm,
Omniscient quietude—the balm
   Of Love's supernal evidence.

Not in the quake, the crash, the heat
Where warring mental forces meet
   Is heard the voice of Truth today.
But in the quiet ministry
Of those who, calm in victory,
   Have learned through Science how to pray.

— *Margaret Morrison*

PRAYER FOR LOVED ONES

I PLACE them in Your hands, dear God;
  I trust them to Your care.
You who mark the sparrow's fall
  And number every hair

Will cherish them and guard them well
  From snares of every kind.
No false responsibility
  Disturbs my peace of mind.

Your love, far greater than my own,
  Provides for them all good.
This have I learned—to humbly trust
  Your father-motherhood.

— Helen C. Benson

Church attendants

WE are His,
    the flock of His good pasture.
Love it is
    that seeks us out, enlightens
    and delivers us,
    gathers, feeds, and folds us,
    values each,
    keeps us safe
    in the gracious place
    of His
    serenely wise and loving
    presence.
We are His,
    the flock of His good pasture.

— Gloria Clements

A PRAYER FOR ONE FAR-OFF

THIS is not releasing, flinging out,
    a human thought, a message of my love,
whirling over the earth's curve,
or through its crust and magma,
nor launching out a wish
to the vagaries of wind,
fragilities of hope,
gestures of human ritual.

No world dimension can arrest,
can touch, can influence,
the perfect functioning of Mind.
There is no here nor there in Spirit's stretch.
Far-off is near, confidence rock-sure.
The reach of Christ is to and all around
each need; and prayer does not produce
but sees this all-sufficient light.

—*Paul Osborne Williams*

PRACTICE

WHEN the waves of fear arose
around that little fishing boat,
where was Jesus?
Walking
out to those he loved
above the water.

Hearing others call for aid
we come and follow unafraid
in Jesus' steps.
Walking
out to those we love
above the water.

—Elizabeth Keyes Williams

Safety

SAFETY*

*H*E whose thought is lifted ever
  To the perfect realm of Mind,
In that secret place abiding
Shall a full protection find.
Safe beneath the Almighty's shade
He shall dwell—all unafraid.

Thousand errors may confront us,
They shall fail on every side,
All our ways are kept by angels,
All our steps they guard and guide.
They who slumber not nor sleep
Day and night their watch shall keep.

They shall show us Love's salvation,
Teach us how to trample fear.
Nothing evil shall befall us
Nor shall any plague come near.
We our Father's name have known,
We will trust in God alone.

— *Violet Hay*

*See Psalm 91

"THE LORD WAS WITH JOSEPH"*

As a child I wondered about Joseph.
How did he know that the Lord was with him?
How could he tell, down there in the dark pit,
In Potiphar's service, and later, in the deep dungeon?
Tides of hatred and envy ran always against him,
There was no certain sign of security,
No response to his universal, friendly outreaching.
How could he be so sure that the Lord was with him?

Have you been cast into depths of despair, yet
    kept your sweetness?
Have you been enslaved by circumstance, yet walked
    as free?
Have you been endungeoned in sorrow, yet comforted
    others?
Forgotten by those you helped, yet not embittered?

Then you have known, like Joseph, that the Lord
    is with you
As the sun is inseparable from the ray expressing it;
And the pit will yield up its victim,
And the dungeon will open its doors,
The servant be served with honor,
And he shall know that the Lord is forever with man,
As man, the beloved, is ever with the Lord.

              — *Rosemary C. Cobham*

*See Genesis 39:2

GOD IS LIGHT

WHAT matter if the night seem dark,
  It is not true;
Your God is where the shadows stark
  Seem circling you.

And God is Love, and in Love's light
  No dream-shades grim
Can keep within a starless night
  His own from Him.

In His dear love no night can be,
  Or ever lo,
He loves throughout eternity.
  And you are His.

—Josephine Hawks

THE PILGRIM

HE who tempers the wind
    To the shorn sheep
Will guard you,
And guide you,
And lead your brave feet
Over the rough ways of the world,
Over crag, over stone;
Up through the clouds,
Through the mist,
And the winds and the cold;
On to the glorified height
To the foot of His throne.
And thus you may know
That He sees you,
And needs you,
And loves you,
And calls you His own.

— *Robert Ellis Key*

SURE MERCIES

SURE mercies
    are mine,
for I am pursued by
God's goodness,
nor could I escape if I would.
Even at the end of the earth or of my rope
He would be there—by His very presence
precluding calamity, unfurling only
the immensity of His love
and the safety of His beloved.

— Carol Chapin Lindsey

SURE DEFENSE

ANOTHER'S thought is his to guard;
And if from heart embittered grown
He send a hurtful thought or word,
The onus, then, is his alone,
And soon or late he must atone.

But I as well must make amend
If, loving self, I let the hurt
Working through my unguarded friend
Rankle and fester in my heart
Till all my peace and love depart.

All-loving Father, holy Mind,
May we, Thy children, one in Thee,
Thy love in all around us find
And peace in loving, so that we
Can neither wound nor wounded be.

— *Rosemary C. Cobham*

Now Is
the Time

NOW IS THE ACCEPTED TIME*

*I*S yesterday still occupying thought?
Can a sense of guilt with backward tilt
Spill the joys today has brought?

Do we dread tomorrow as bringing some sorrow,
Confusion or lack
To hold us back?

Oh, why need we borrow from past or tomorrow
Yesterday's tears
Or evil's false fears?

When by turning to Mind, right now we can find
Release from past woe;
And letting it go

Claim our dominion in God's promised way:
That each error revealed
By Truth will be healed
In the *now* of God's eternal day.

— *Helen Oscar Winfield*

*See II Corinthians 6:2

THE GATE CALLED
BEAUTIFUL*

ODAY the sentinels are unaware
    At the gate called Beautiful a host is heeding
The ancient dialogue left on the air—
Peter's response, at the gate, to the lame man's pleading:
"Silver and gold have I none; but such as I have
Give I thee: In the name of Jesus Christ of Nazareth
Rise up and walk." And he was healed. But the waves
Of the sound widened out into silence then; the path
Lost purpose; the keepers closed and locked that gate.
A Messiah will come—they rehearsed the ancient vow—
To open wide its doors; let the centuries wait.
But the gate called Beautiful is open now.
    For blind men see, and deaf and dumb men talk,
    In the name of Jesus Christ—we rise and walk.

—*Margaret Hovenden Ogden*

*See Acts 3:1-10

INSTANT IMAGE

WHEN you stand before the mirror,
   You do not have to wait
To see your counterpart appear,
   Or glass elucidate.

Nor does God wait for you
   To reach a slow perfection.
Existing now, at one with Him,
   You are instantly *reflection*.

—*Donna Virgil Holden*

Rise now

WAITED
and waited
(like the man at the pool of Bethesda)
for an angel
to come and move the waters
of my thought.

But then God said:
"Don't wait … rise now!"

So as I looked
with my heart I found
that His angels were all around!
And, as I rose, they took my hand
and tenderly
led me on.

— Faith Walsh Heidtbrink

No delay

*J*UST as a room though dark for years
    We change at once by flood of light,
So error claiming darkest past
Truth instantly can put to flight.

                    — *Elizabeth Bice Luerssen*

To see God

*"Blessed are the pure in heart: for they shall see God."**

N O need for waiting.
   Today walk
in white-robed selflessness.
Live the prayer
that penetrates matter's sham.
With confidence
   in God's allness/goodness
   go forth
to see the universe
   as He made it;
to find in place of want
   His promises fulfilled;
to look into prisons
   (of sickness/sin)
         and behold the face
            of innocence.

— Mary Martin Odell

A SONG OF HOPE

HITHERTO the Lord hath helped us
As we faltered on life's way.
Hitherto His arm hath held us;
Can we doubt His love today?

Hitherto hath Love sustained us—
Let us not forget the years
Filled with fruitage of His goodness;
Grateful praise should heal our fears.

Hitherto God's truth has led us
Safely through each hour of need,
For He changeth not nor faileth—
Precious promises to heed!

Hitherto hath Life unfolded
Man hid safe in God alway!
Hitherto the Lord hath helped us—
Trust in Him! rejoice today!

— Minny M. H. Ayers

AUTHOR INDEX

NOTE: Original publications are noted below and abbreviated as follows:
Christian Science Sentinel is *CSS* and *The Christian Science Journal* is *CSJ*.

Lubin, Doris
The wedding, 28
(Originally published *CSS*, March 21, 1988)

Luerssen, Elizabeth Bice
I'd rather give audience to Spirit, 37
(Originally published *CSJ*, May 1988)
No delay, 113
(Originally published *CSS*, March 1, 1952)

MacDonald, Bonnie
"The truth shall make you free," 93
(Originally published *CSS*, September 25, 2006)

Morrison, Margaret
The voice of Truth, 94
(Originally published *CSJ*, April 1950)

Odell, Mary Martin
(*later* DeShaw)
To see God, 114
(Originally published *CSJ*, September 1961)

Ogden, Margaret Hovenden
The gate called Beautiful, 110
(Originally published *CSS*, April 5, 1969)

Phinney, Allison W.
I can tell you this…, 90
(Originally published *CSS*, January 19, 2009)
Such a difference, 60
(Originally published *CSS*, October 15, 2007)

Quinn, Doris Kerns
Joy frees, 88
(Originally published *CSS*, August 4, 1994)
The single eye, 29
(Originally published *CSS*, June 25, 1984)
Thoroughness, 59
(Originally published *CSJ*, July 1991)

Robinson, E. Jewel
Desire, 61
(Originally published *CSS*, February 14, 1925)
"Desire is prayer", 80
(Originally published *CSS*, October 8, 1932)

Rogers, Harold
Be still, my heart, 30
(Originally published *CSJ*, July 1987)

Schiering, Geraldine
Noble endeavor, 31
(Originally published *CSS*, June 9, 1997)

Scott, Beverly Jean
Integrity's quiet question, 62
(Originally published *CSJ*, January 1977)

Scott, Virginia L.
The garment of gratitude, 46
(Originally published *CSJ*, November 1985)

Slaughter, Cora
Your testimony, 40
(Originally published *CSS*, July 3, 1978)

Stafford, Brett L.
Just what is healing?, 64
(Originally published *CSJ*, August 1980)

Stewart, Ann C.
Home, 41
(Originally published *CSJ*, September 1966)

Thwaites, Alan W.
Counsel, 66
(Originally published *CSS*, July 22, 1972)

Tis, Marjorie Russell
Homecoming, 67
(Originally published *CSJ*, September 1999)

Williams, Elizabeth Keyes
Practice, 98
(Originally published *CSS*, September 13, 1982)

Williams, Paul Osborne
A prayer for one far-off, 97
(Originally published *CSS*, December 3, 1979)

Winfield, Helen Oscar
Now is the accepted time, 109
(Originally published *CSS*, September 4, 1971)

POEM TITLE INDEX